PEOPLE AT THE CENTER OF

WORLD WAR II

By AUDREY KUPFERBERG

BLACKBIRCH™
PRESS

THOMSON
GALE

San Diego • Detroit • New York • San Francisco • Cleveland
New Haven, Conn. • Waterville, Maine • London • Munich

THOMSON

✴

™

GALE

LIBRARY OF CONGRESS CATALOGING-IN-PUBLICATION DATA

Kupferberg, Audrey E.
  World War II / by Audrey Kupferberg.
    p. cm. — (People at the center of:)
  Summary: Profiles people involved in World War II, including both political and military leaders on both sides of the conflict.
  Includes bibliographical references.
  ISBN 1-56711-774-0 (hardback : alk. paper)
  1. World War, 1939-1945—Biography—Juvenile literature. [1. World War, 1939-1945—Biography.] I. Title: World War Two. II. Title: World War 2. III. Title. IV. Series.

  D736.K85 2004
  940.53'092'2—dc21   2003010093

Printed in United States
10 9 8 7 6 5 4 3 2 1

Contents

WORLD WAR II

The seeds that eventually sprouted into World War II were planted two decades earlier, at the end of World War I (1914–1918). In that conflict, the Central Powers, consisting of Germany and Austria-Hungary, were defeated by the Allies, primarily made up of France, Britain, Russia, and, later, the United States. The war ended with the Treaty of Versailles, signed in 1919, which stripped Germany of its colonies and diminished its military force. The country was forced to pay massive financial reparations to the victors. Germany emerged a dispirited nation, plagued by unemployment and economic chaos.

Of the many heroes and villains associated with World War II, the most prominent is Adolf Hitler. During the early 1920s, Hitler became head of the National Socialist (Nazi) Party, which throughout the decade steadily increased its influence in Germany. He was a brilliant orator, and in his speeches he blamed Germany's ills on the world's Jewish population. In 1933, Hitler became Chancellor of Germany. He promptly started a campaign of discrimination against Germany's Jews and stripped them of their rights as citizens.

Hitler built up Germany's industries in preparation for war, and started to invade and annex, or take over, surrounding nations. On September 1, 1939, Hitler's armies invaded Poland. Britain, France, Australia, and New Zealand declared war against Germany. Many nations divided into two opposing powers: the Allies and the Axis. The Allies consisted of twenty-five countries that were opposed to Hitler, including Britain, Russia, China, and later, the United States. The primary Axis powers were Germany, Italy, and Japan.

During the war, Italy was headed by the dictator Benito Mussolini. In June 1940, Mussolini declared war on France and Britain. At first, Germany and Italy won victory upon victory. In May–June 1940, more than 330,000 British and Allied

Adolf Hitler was head of the Nazi Party and chancellor of Germany. He launched invasions of neighboring European countries and ignited World War II.

After the attack on Pearl Harbor on December 7, 1941, the United States declared war on Japan, and later on Germany and Italy as well.

troops were evacuated from Dunkerque (Dunkirk), a northern French seaport on the English Channel. On June 14, German forces marched into Paris, and France fell to the Axis powers.

Between August and October 1940, Britain's Royal Air Force (RAF) and Germany's air force, called the Luftwaffe, faced off in an air battle known as the Battle of Britain. Despite being severely outmanned, the RAF won. This victory permanently postponed Hitler's planned invasion of Britain. Then in June 1941, Germany ignored a nonaggression pact it previously had signed and invaded Russia.

On December 7, 1941, the war expanded after Japan made a surprise attack on the U.S. naval fleet at Pearl Harbor, Hawaii, in which eight U.S. battleships were bombed. The following day, the United States and Britain declared war on Japan. Two days later, Germany and Italy declared war on the United States.

Despite its weakened naval power as a result of the Pearl Harbor bombing, the United States won its first victories during the spring of 1942, in the Coral Sea northeast of Australia and in the Pacific Ocean at Midway, a group of islands twelve hundred miles northwest of Honolulu, Hawaii. That fall, the Allies pushed back the Germans at El Alamein in North Africa. Early in 1943, the Russians turned back the Germans at Stalingrad, one of Russia's major industrial cities. In June, Sicily, a large Mediterranean island that is part of Italy, fell to the Allies. Mussolini was forced from power and, in September, Italy surrendered to the Allies.

During the war, Hitler imprisoned in concentration camps European Jews, political dissenters, Communists, gypsies, homosexuals, and anyone deemed undesirable by the German state. The camps started out as slave labor camps but many evolved into death camps, which were the final destinations of approximately 12 million individuals who were tortured, shot, or murdered in gas chambers.

The final stage of the war in Europe began on June 6, 1944, known as D-day. On that date, 2,727 Allied vessels—the largest fleet of all

Hitler forced Jews and others he deemed inferior into concentration camps where millions died. Pictured here are two prisoners at the Buchenwald concentration camp.

time—sailed to Normandy on the northwest coast of Nazi-occupied France. By September, most of the German armies were driven out of France and Belgium. After France's liberation, a temporary government took power. Allied forces next stormed into Germany. In December 1944, the Germans failed at their final counteroffensive in the Battle of the Bulge.

In April 1945, Mussolini was killed by Italian fighters who supported the Allies. That same month, Hitler committed suicide in his bunker in Berlin, Germany's capital city. That spring, representatives of fifty-six nations attended the San Francisco Conference, which resulted in the formation of the United Nations: a forum for discussing and settling future disputes between nations.

Left: The atomic bombs dropped on Hiroshima and Nagasaki (pictured) led to Japan's surrender. Above: The Berlin Wall separated East Germany from West Germany for decades after World War II.

Meanwhile, the Allies had been attacking and taking over Japanese-held islands in the Pacific Ocean and were poised for an invasion of Japan. The assault was not necessary. In August 1945, the United States dropped atomic bombs over Hiroshima and Nagasaki, Japan. On September 2, Japan surrendered to the Allies. World War II was at an end. More than 52 million persons worldwide had lost their lives during the conflict.

Between 1945 and 1949, a series of war crimes trials were held in Nuremberg, Germany. Nazi leaders—those who had not committed suicide at war's end—were accused of planning and waging war, killing or abusing civilians and prisoners of war, destroying communities, looting property, and enslaving or murdering individuals based on racial, political, or religious background.

In 1949, Germany was divided into two countries. East Germany (the German Democratic Republic) was under the control of of Russia. West Germany (the Federal Republic of Germany) was an independent democracy. The two were reunited as one country in 1990.

After the surrender of Japan, that country was occupied by U.S. troops. In 1946, a new, democratic constitution was presented. Japan again became an independent nation in 1951.

Adolf Hitler

Launched World War II

Adolf Hitler was born in 1889 in Braunau, Austria. Before World War I (1914–1918), he spent six years in Vienna where he was practically penniless. He became interested in politics, developed his skills as a public speaker, and embraced anti-Semitism, the hatred of Jews. During World War I, he served in the German military.

In 1919, Hitler became a member of the right-wing German Workers' Party, which evolved into the National Socialist (Nazi) Party. Then in 1923, he unsuccessfully tried to take over the government of Bavaria, a region of Germany, and was convicted of attempting to overthrow a seated government. During a nine-month prison term, he authored *Mein Kampf* (My Struggle), in which he conveyed his desire to transform Germany into a world power. By the beginning of World War II, *Mein Kampf* had sold 5 million copies.

Above: Adolf Hitler was a powerful orator. Opposite: Hitler addressed the Reichstag on October 6, 1939, a little more than a month after he launched the invasion of Poland.

Hitler combined his skills as a powerful orator and his ability to manipulate the masses to transform the Nazi Party into a potent political movement. Germans by the thousands were aroused by Hitler's call for the establishment of a great German empire. By 1932, the Nazis had become Germany's dominant party and, the following year, Hitler became Germany's chancellor. He strengthened his power by exterminating his party adversaries and began a campaign of discrimination against German Jews. He also started to build up Germany's industries, to prepare for war.

Soon, Hitler began to occupy surrounding regions, which included the Rhineland (1936), Austria (1938), and Czechoslovakia (1939). On September 1, 1939, his armies invaded Poland and, as a result, England and France declared war on Germany. This is widely considered the start of World War II.

Hitler's military strategy was nearly flawless until he ordered the invasion of Russia in 1941, which violated a nonaggression pact he signed with Russia two years earlier. Hitler's armies were unable to effectively attack and defend on both the Russian and European fronts. Eventually, his armies were repelled after the Allied invasion of Nazi-occupied Europe, which commenced on the beaches of Normandy on June 6, 1944.

On April 30, 1945, with the war all but lost, Hitler committed suicide. His body was never found.

PAUL JOSEPH GOEBBELS

HITLER'S MINISTER OF PROPAGANDA

Joseph Goebbels was born in Rheydt, Germany, in 1897. He was rejected by the German army during World War I (1914–1918) because of a physical disability. A brilliant student, he earned a doctor of philosophy degree from Heidelberg University in southwestern Germany. In the 1920s, he joined the National Socialist (Nazi) Party and met Adolf Hitler.

Hitler was taken with Goebbels's talent as an orator and writer and his ability to use words to play on the fears of the masses. Both men agreed that the written word and moving image could be employed as powerful tools to spread their political ideas.

In 1926, Goebbels became a Nazi Party district leader in Berlin; around that time, he founded and wrote for *Der Angriff* (Attack), a weekly newspaper that put forth Nazi Party propaganda. Then in 1928, he was one of eleven party members elected to the Reichstag, Germany's lower governmental house.

When Hitler became chancellor in 1933, Goebbels was named Germany's minister for public enlightenment and propaganda. He was responsible for organizing massive political rallies that presented Hitler as redeemer of the Germany people. Goebbels's position allowed him total control of the content of all German

Opposite: Joseph Goebbels led rallies to garner support for Hitler prior to and during the war. Above: Goebbels (left) and Hitler both had plans for a new and powerful Germany.

media, from films and theater productions to newspapers and radio broadcasts. He manipulated these media outlets to publicize Nazism across Germany and fan hatred against the Jews. Once the war began, Goebbels employed his talent for promoting propaganda to rally the German citizenry to join the war effort.

In 1945, when Soviet troops were about to enter Berlin and it was clear that the war was lost, Goebbels, his wife, and six children committed suicide.

HEINRICH HIMMLER

HEAD OF THE SS AND THE GESTAPO

Heinrich Himmler was born in Munich in 1900. He fought in the German army during World War I (1914–1918) and, in 1923, he participated in the failed attempt by Adolf Hitler to overthrow the German government.

Next to Adolf Hitler, Himmler was the most powerful man in Nazi Germany. In 1929, he became head of the Schutzstaffel (SS), which served primarily as Hitler's personal bodyguards. At the time, the SS consisted of between two hundred and three hundred men. By 1933, Himmler had expanded the SS to include more than fifty thousand members. In 1936, he was named head of the Geheime Staatspolizei (secret police), commonly known as the Gestapo. The power of the Gestapo was practically unlimited. Any German citizen suspected of disloyalty to Hitler could be arrested and executed, without benefit of a trial, or dispatched to one of the forced labor camps established by Himmler.

Above: Heinrich Himmler oversaw the concentration camps, in which 12 million people were killed. Opposite: Himmler served as Hitler's right-hand man and headed the Gestapo throughout the war.

Himmler was a master strategist in the genocide of Jews and other minority groups that were deemed unacceptable by the Nazi Party. Initially, Himmler's concentration camps housed state prisoners and were located throughout Germany.

Eventually, more concentration camps were established in the countries that Hitler was annexing. As head of the Gestapo, Himmler was charged with overseeing all these camps. Some became death camps. Treblinka, Auschwitz, Buchenwald, and Dachau were among the most notorious. Six million Jews and an equal number of non-Jews died in concentration camps.

In 1945, as defeat seemed forthcoming, Himmler became chief of the Volksturm, a hastily assembled army of adolescents and elderly men whose unlikely mission was to be the final line of defense against the Allies. After Germany's defeat, Himmler was captured by the British and committed suicide while in custody.

BENITO MUSSOLINI

FASCIST DICTATOR OF ITALY

Benito Mussolini was born in Predappio, Italy, in 1883. As a young man, he was an avid socialist—one who believes that all land, money, and manufacturing concerns should be controlled by the community rather than the individual. By the end of World War I, he had abandoned socialism and embraced the tenets of fascism. He believed that the future of Italy lay in the establishment of a government headed by an all-powerful dictator who would aggressively curb all opposition and control all trade and industry. His dream was to create, and be the ruler of, an Italian empire.

After World War I, Italy was rife with economic and political unrest. In 1919, Mussolini established a fascist political faction in Milan, and his group attracted thousands of supporters who were dissatisfied with the widespread disorder in their country. Mussolini organized the Fascist Party in 1921, and became *il duce* (leader); his armed gangs now intimidated his old socialist associates.

The next year, Mussolini's private army marched into Rome, which resulted in Italy's king Victor Emmanuel III naming him the nation's premier. Immediately he censored opposing ideas and took control of the press, radio, motion pictures, and the educational system. By 1925, he had outlawed all other

Opposite: Benito Mussolini aligned himself with Hitler and declared war on the Allies during World War II. Above: Allied forces liberated Rome in 1944.

political parties and become dictator of Italy. He then focused on the annexation of other nations. In 1935–1936, he occupied Ethiopia. In 1939, he took possession of Albania. He linked up politically with Adolf Hitler and, in 1940, declared war on the Allied powers.

His military forces, however, were ill-equipped to participate in such a widespread war. His armies were defeated in Greece, North Africa, and, eventually, on their home turf. In 1943, Mussolini's Italy was in chaos, and his political power was nil. German forces were battling the Allies, who already controlled southern Italy.

Mussolini established a puppet regime (a government that is set up and controlled by an outside country) in German-controlled northern Italy, which eventually fell to the Allies. In April 1945, he was killed by Italian supporters of the Allies.

Emperor Hirohito was born in Tokyo in 1901; his birth name was Michinomiya. His father was Emperor Yoshihito, and his mother was an empress-princess. In 1914, he completed his studies at the Gakushuin (Peers' School) and two years later was named Japan's crown prince. Upon Yoshihito's death in 1926, Hirohito became the 124th emperor of Japan. At the time, Japanese emperors were looked upon as gods and absolute rulers.

From the late 1920s on, Japan was determined to expand its rule throughout Asia and annex other countries. Most infamously, it invaded Manchuria, a region in northeastern China, and later moved into China. In 1940, Japan joined Germany and Italy in the Axis alliance. Japan entered World War II in December 1941 with its surprise attack on the U.S. naval base at Pearl Harbor, Hawaii.

Hirohito's exact role in Japan's hostile actions remains subject to speculation. One version is that, shortly after he assumed his country's throne, a group of militarists gained control of the Japanese government and implemented Japan's increasingly aggressive foreign policy. By another account, Hirohito was an active participant in the execution of this policy and allegedly was among the planners of the Pearl Harbor attack.

The role of Japanese emperor Hirohito (opposite page) in World War II is surrounded with controversy. He continued to lead the country even after U.S. atomic bombs exploded over Hiroshima and Nagasaki (above).

Japan surrendered to the Allies in 1945 after the U.S. atomic bomb attacks on Hiroshima and Nagasaki. Unlike the other Axis leaders, Hirohito was not viewed as a war criminal. Instead, he was looked upon as a pawn of Japan's militarists. Furthermore, U.S. general Douglas MacArthur, who was directing the Allied occupation of Japan, believed that an orderly occupation was possible only if Hirohito remained in power.

After the war, Hirohito came to be viewed as a mortal rather than a god. A new constitution of 1947 decreed that emperors no longer had political power; their positions would be largely ceremonial. Japan remained occupied by U.S. forces until 1951, when complete independence and self-rule were restored. Hirohito remained emperor of Japan until his death in 1989.

ARTHUR NEVILLE CHAMBERLAIN

AGREED TO HITLER'S DEMANDS

Arthur Neville Chamberlain hailed from a prominent British political family. He was born in 1869 in Birmingham, an industrial city in central Britain, and attended Rugby and Mason College. In 1918, he was elected to the British Parliament. He became his country's prime minister in 1937.

At the time, Adolf Hitler was aggressively occupying nations on the European continent. Chamberlain became concerned that Germany would one day attempt to extend its reach to Britain. Determined to avoid such a catastrophe, Chamberlain decided to follow a policy of appeasement, or keeping the peace by giving into some of Hitler's demands.

British prime minister Arthur Neville Chamberlain (opposite page) gave in to Hitler's demands at the 1938 Munich Conference (above) in a failed attempt to avoid war.

Most notoriously, Chamberlain gave in to Hitler at Munich, in the Bavarian region of Germany, in September 1938. Here, he and French premier Édouard Daladier signed the Munich Agreement, which was an attempt to avoid war by surrendering the industry-rich Sudetenland of western Czechoslovakia to Nazi Germany. Czechoslovakia was a militarily and governmentally weak nation that was held in little regard by the French and British. Therefore, even though France and England had no legal right to give part of Czechoslovakia to Hitler, they chose to do so anyway. The following month, German armies occupied the Sudetenland and the government of Czechoslovakia resigned.

Chamberlain hoped that the terms of the Munich Agreement would satisfy Hitler and convince him to curtail his expansionist policies. Upon his return to Britain, he announced triumphantly that Germany and Britain "are determined to continue our efforts to remove possible sources of difference, and thus to contribute to assure the peace of Europe." He added, "My good friends . . . I believe it is peace for our time."

This was not to be. When Hitler broke the Munich Agreement by seizing the rest of Czechoslovakia in March 1939, Chamberlain realized that his policy of appeasement had failed. This became even more evident upon Hitler's invasion of Poland in September. Two days later, Britain declared war on Germany.

Chamberlain resigned from office in May 1940 and was replaced by Winston Churchill. He died six months later.

WINSTON CHURCHILL

INSPIRED AND LED GREAT BRITAIN

Born in 1874 at Blenheim Palace, about an hour's drive from London, to a political family, Winston Churchill attended Harrow, a respected English boarding school, and graduated from the Royal Military College at Sandhurst. After a brief career as an army officer and war correspondent, Churchill followed his father into politics.

When Adolf Hitler took control of Germany in 1933, Churchill was among the first to recognize the Nazi dictator as an international threat. As a student of European history, Churchill saw a dangerous pattern in Hitler's public speeches, in which he stated his intentions to place the nations of Europe under Nazi control. Churchill believed that the European continent never should become dominated by a single dictator; and for that reason alone, to ensure the balance of world power, Hitler must not be allowed to take over Europe. Churchill warned the British government to prepare for a possible war with Germany, but the British leaders responded with disbelief.

When war did break out in September 1939, Churchill was reappointed first lord of admiralty, a position to which he had initially been appointed in 1911. The following year, Prime Minister Neville Chamberlain was forced to resign for his past attempts to keep the peace by giving in to Hitler's demands. He was replaced by Churchill, who held the leadership post until 1945.

Churchill proved to be an outstanding wartime prime minister who refused to bend to Hitler. Where Chamberlain attempted to pacify Hitler, Churchill ordered that bombs be dropped on Germany. In a series of powerful speeches, he revived the sunken spirit of the British people, who were suffering under the pressure of bombings and loved ones endangered in battles. In one instance of skilled war planning, Churchill convinced American president Franklin Roosevelt that a large number of British and American troops should be sent to North Africa to overpower the Axis forces in the area.

After the war, a misplay in politics cost Churchill and his party reelection; however, he served again as prime minister from 1951 to 1955. For his six-volume, postwar account, *The Second World War*, he was awarded the Nobel Prize in literature. Churchill died in 1965.

Opposite: British prime minister Winston Churchill (center, with cigar) revitalized the spirit of the British people, stood strong against Hitler, and ordered the retaliatory bombing of Germany.

Joseph Stalin

Brought Russia into the alliance

Joseph Stalin was born Iosif Vissarionovich Dzhugashvili in 1879 in Gori, a village in central Georgia, under Russian control. While a young Communist, he changed his name to Stalin (Russian for "man of steel"). In 1929, he became his country's ruler and transformed Russian communism from a revolutionary peoples' movement to a rigid, bureaucratic dictatorship. His regime was characterized by the widespread jailing and execution of his political rivals, and of those who disagreed with his policies.

In his foreign policy, Stalin was as equally brutal as Adolf Hitler. The two became allied when, in August 1939, they signed a nonaggression pact. The following month, Stalin authorized the invasion of Poland by Russia two weeks after German armies marched into the country. Russia and Germany then divided up the conquered nation. Also in 1939, Stalin invaded Finland and forced Communist leadership on the Baltic States (Latvia, Lithuania, and Estonia).

Russian dictator Joseph Stalin (opposite) worked with the British and American leaders (above) to defeat Hitler in World War II.

Stalin's agreement with Hitler was nullified in June 1941, when Germany suddenly invaded Russia. Stalin then personally took full control of the Russian military. Through the end of the war, he and a small group of advisers decided on all military and political strategies. Meanwhile, Russian cities fell one by one to the Nazis. The tide finally was reversed in February 1943, when the Germans were turned back at Stalingrad.

Between 1943 and 1945, Stalin met with his British and American counterparts in a series of conferences in which they plotted strategy, offered ultimatums for surrender to the Axis, and debated the way in which Germany and Japan would be dealt with after the war. Upon the Allied victory, Russia occupied most of the Eastern European countries and one area of Germany. Stalinist governments eventually were installed in the Eastern European nations and, in 1949, the eastern part of Germany became the German Democratic Republic, a Communist-ruled satellite of Russia.

Stalin remained in power in Russia until his sudden death in 1953.

(Henri-) Philippe Pétain

Cooperated with German occupiers

(Henri-) Philippe Pétain was born in Cauchy-la-Tour, two hundred miles south of Paris, in 1856. He attended the Ecole Militaire (Military Academy) of Saint-Cyr-l'École and spent decades as an army officer. He became one of his nation's heroes during World War I (1914–1918) and was his country's minister of war in 1934.

Pétain believed in employing a defensive military strategy against Hitler. He backed construction of the Maginot Line, an enormous French defense system made up of attached underground forts that was constructed between 1934 and 1940 along the Swiss and Belgian borders. It extended from Switzerland to the Ardennes plateau region in the north, and from the Alps to the Mediterranean in the south. The line was outdated even before its construction was finished because it was too short, and, it did not stand up against the powerful tanks and dive-bomber aircraft of modern Nazi warfare. As a result, the line was sidestepped by the German armies as they invaded France.

Two days after Hitler's armies marched into Paris in 1940, Pétain was named France's premier. Instead of going into exile and continuing to fight the Germans, Pétain believed that such a struggle would be futile and signed an armistice with the Nazis. From then on, the French government collaborated with the Nazi occupiers by providing them with properties, goods, and services. Pétain's aim was to ensure a significant political role for his country after what he expected to be a German victory.

Almost immediately, France severed its ties with Britain; Pétain even personally met with Hitler and pledged his collaboration. His government was powerless, however, and merely served as a puppet for Hitler. Pétain's regime was known as the Vichy government because it was seated not in Paris but in Vichy, a health resort in south central France.

After the Allied offensive that began on D-day, Pétain left France. Upon his return in 1945, he was arrested and accused of treason. He was found guilty of assisting the Nazis and sentenced to death, which was commuted to life in prison. He died in prison in 1951.

Opposite Page: French premier Philipe Pétain cooperated with Hitler after Germany invaded France. He headed what amounted to a puppet government in Vichy during the war.

CHARLES DE GAULLE

Charles de Gaulle was born in Lille, France, in 1890. He attended the Ecole Militaire (Military Academy) of Saint-Cyr-l'École ,and was wounded and captured by the Germans while fighting in World War I (1914–1918). After the war, he wrote books and articles on military history and served in various posts in the French military and government.

At the beginning of World War II in 1939, de Gaulle was a military field commander. In that capacity, he tried to halt the German armies as they marched into France. By June 1940, when France fell to Germany, de Gaulle had been named his country's minister for national defense and war. Unlike most French cabinet members, he opposed surrendering to the Germans. Instead, he suggested that the government reform itself outside the country and work to thwart the invaders.

De Gaulle's proposal was ignored by (Henri-) Philippe Pétain, France's new premier. Pétain signed an armistice (a temporary halt in hostilities) with the Nazis, and from then on, the presiding French government aided the Nazis. After he escaped to England, de Gaulle spoke on the radio and appealed to his countrymen and women to resist the Nazis. He then formed the Free French movement and began to organize an army of fighters to return to France to battle the Germans. Meanwhile, back home, a French court sentenced him to death for the crime of treason.

De Gaulle eventually established contact with the French Resistance, an underground movement in which citizens still living in France were attempting to thwart the Germans. More than any other individual, he symbolized France's resistance against the Germans.

In 1944, the Allies marched through France and liberated the country. Because of his earlier position with the last French government to be formally recognized by the British, the British accepted de Gaulle as head of the provisional (temporary) French government. He announced plans to jump-start the nation's industry and organize free elections, which reestablished self-esteem among the French people.

De Gaulle resigned his post in 1946 after internal disagreement in the composition of a postwar French government constitution. He later served as France's president between 1958 and 1969. He died in 1970.

Opposite Page: Charles de Gaulle was a symbol of the French resistance to German occupation in France. He established the Free French movement to take back the country and later served as president of France.

FRANKLIN D. ROOSEVELT

LED AMERICA THROUGH MUCH OF THE WAR

Franklin Delano Roosevelt was born in 1882 at Hyde Park, New York. He attended Harvard University and Columbia University Law School. In 1928, he was elected governor of New York. He became president of the United States in 1932 and won reelection an unprecedented three times.

In September 1939, World War II began after Hitler's armies invaded Poland. Roosevelt's desire was to keep the United States out of the conflict. Days after war was declared, the United States announced its neutrality. The side it favored, however, was clearly evident. In March 1941, the United States and the European Allies signed the Lend-Lease Act, in which the United States agreed to send them all possible aid short of troops.

U.S. neutrality ceased on December 7, 1941, when the Japanese launched a surprise attack on an American military base at Pearl Harbor, Hawaii. Now, Roosevelt had no choice but to command the country through another world war. By December 11, the United States was at war against Japan, Germany, and Italy. Roosevelt ordered that all U.S. assets and manpower be devoted to fighting and winning the war. In one of his most famous speeches, he referred to December 7 as "a date that will live in infamy."

Roosevelt forged a strong, unbending alliance with the Allied powers. Throughout the war, he regularly conferred with Britain's Winston Churchill and Russia's Joseph Stalin on war strategy. They proposed detailed plans for the surrender of the Axis powers and

U.S. president Franklin D. Roosevelt (opposite) originally sought to keep America out of the war. After the Japanese attack on Pearl Harbor, however, he joined with the other Allied leaders (above) to fight the Axis powers.

discussed the manner in which Germany and Japan would be dealt with upon the war's end. Roosevelt also was concerned for the future of world peace. To this end, he devoted much effort to the establishment of the United Nations.

Roosevelt did not live to see the end of World War II. In April 1945, he died suddenly while resting at his retreat in Warm Springs, Georgia.

Douglas MacArthur

The son of a distinguished U.S. Army officer, Douglas MacArthur was born in Little Rock, Arkansas, in 1880. He ranked first in his class at the United States Military Academy at West Point in southeastern New York State. During World War I (1914–1918), MacArthur was decorated for his courage in battle. After the war, he became superintendent of West Point and served in a number of key military advisory positions in the United States and the Philippines.

General Douglas MacArthur (opposite page) was integral in the liberation of the Philippines. He later played a key role in the management of Japan after it surrendered to Allied powers (above) in 1945.

In the early weeks of U.S. participation in World War II, MacArthur failed to maintain a defense of the Philippines, which had been a colony of the United States from 1898 to 1935 and the recipient of substantial U.S. investment. In spite of this defeat, President Franklin Roosevelt trusted MacArthur's ability. He promoted MacArthur from commander of U.S. forces in the Far East to the rank of supreme commander of the Allied forces in the southwest Pacific.

MacArthur's first objective was to overtake the Japanese, who controlled many large islands in the Pacific Ocean. To do so, he devised a plan to land Allied troops on the islands that were not occupied by the Japanese, in order to establish military bases near the enemy. Once aircraft and munitions were available to troops at these bases, the soldiers were able to attack and occupy the Japanese-held islands. It was in this manner that MacArthur and his armies eventually returned to, and liberated, the Philippines.

Next came a struggle to control Okinawa, a key port from which to launch an assault on Japan. Finally, Okinawa was taken. MacArthur prepared to invade Japan. He would have done so; however, President Harry Truman ordered atomic bombs to be dropped on Hiroshima and Nagasaki, which virtually ended World War II.

As general of the Allied armies, MacArthur accepted the surrender of Japan aboard the battleship USS *Missouri* on September 2, 1945. He later directed the Allied occupation of Japan. MacArthur died in 1964.

George S. Patton

Brilliant military strategist

Controversial U.S. general George Patton was born in San Gabriel, California, in 1885, and graduated from the United States Military Academy at West Point in southeastern New York State. During World War I (1914–1918), he was in charge of the 304th Tank Brigade and was wounded while fighting in France.

When the United States entered World War II, Patton had risen to the rank of brigadier general and was commander of the 2nd Armored Division at Fort Benning, Georgia. Soon, he was devising military strategy and leading his men to victory against the Axis forces. In 1942, as commander of the Western Task Force, he and his troops were dispatched to North Africa and liberated Morocco from the Nazis. Then he helped prepare for the invasion of Sicily. He played a major role in leading the 7th Army on the battlefield during this successful campaign, a victory that resulted in Italy's withdrawal from the war.

Patton was a brilliant military strategist but a flawed leader. His victory in Italy was stained when, in two highly publicized episodes, he slapped a private who had been afflicted with battle fatigue, and he also waved a pistol at another similarly afflicted soldier. These incidents disqualified him from higher command. Patton's skill as a military strategist, however, could not be ignored, and in 1944 he was made commander of the 3rd Army. In this capacity, Patton successfully led U.S. forces on an offensive across Nazi-occupied France. Under Patton, U.S. troops swiftly advanced from Normandy to Brittany and northern France, then took over Bastogne and crossed the Rhine River into southern Germany and Czechoslovakia.

After the war in Europe ended, Patton was named military governor of Bavaria, a large cultural and industrial area in southeastern Germany. He was entrusted with overseeing the redevelopment of this important part of Germany. Here, too, he courted controversy when he permitted Nazis to stay in political office. He was relieved of his command and ordered to take charge of the Allied 15th Army Group in the U.S.–occupied section of West Germany.

In December 1945, just before he was scheduled to return to the United States, Patton died in an automobile accident.

Opposite Page: General George S. Patton was a brilliant military strategist who led U.S. forces in several important victories against Axis powers during World War II.

DWIGHT D. EISENHOWER

SUPREME ALLIED COMMANDER

Dwight Eisenhower was born in Denison, Texas, in 1890, and graduated from the United States Military Academy at West Point in southeastern New York State. Through the beginning of World War II, he served as a tank brigade commander and on the staffs at military posts in the United States, Panama, France, and the Philippines.

Just after Pearl Harbor, Eisenhower was called to assist in planning the war against Germany and Japan. In early 1942, he was dispatched to England to head the U.S. forces in the European theater of operations (the combat and communications zones of a military operation or war). Soon, he was chosen as the Allied commander for the invasion of North Africa. After a lengthy series of battles, the Allies emerged victorious. By then a full general, Eisenhower planned and oversaw the invasions of Sicily and mainland Italy. On September 8, 1943, he was the presiding American military officer during the Italian surrender to the Allies. The Germans, however, kept fighting in Italy. In early 1944, Eisenhower and his fellow strategists directed the Allies to attack the Germans at Cassino and Anzio.

U.S. president Franklin Roosevelt and British prime minister Winston Churchill had come to respect Eisenhower for his ability to lead soldiers from varied countries. It was for this reason that he was named supreme commander of the Allied Expeditionary Force, and was charged with overseeing the Allied invasion of Europe.

Opposite: General Dwight D. Eisenhower was supreme allied commander. Above: Eisenhower and his commanders oversaw the Allied strategy that defeated the Axis powers.

Eisenhower's job was to organize 1 million combat troops and an additional 2 million support troops. The invasion began on June 6, 1944, when the Allies landed at Normandy. The Allies suffered thousands of casualties, but the invasion was an astounding success and resulted in the German surrender. It was Eisenhower's greatest wartime triumph.

Eisenhower retired from the military in 1948. Four years later, he was elected president of the United States. Eisenhower won reelection in 1956, left office in 1961, and died eight years later.

(ANNA) ELEANOR ROOSEVELT

IMPROVED AMERICAN MORALE AT HOME AND ABROAD

Eleanor Roosevelt was born in New York City in 1884. She married her distant cousin, Franklin D. Roosevelt, in 1905 and became the nation's first lady when he was elected U.S. president in 1932. She changed the established role of the first lady from hostess to social reformer and ambassador, and she was an eloquent spokesperson for the president's policies.

First lady Eleanor Roosevelt (opposite page) was an active participant in World War II. She gave speeches, led the Office of Civilian Defense, visited U.S. troops (above), and urged integration in several military organizations.

In 1941, when America's entry into World War II seemed to be a possibility, Roosevelt became an administrator of the newly created Office of Civilian Defense (OCD). The responsibility of the OCD was to shield America's civilian population in case of war, preserve the nation's morale, and encourage volunteer participation in the nation's defense. Roosevelt was criticized for some of the staff appointments she made and for her attempts to racially integrate the OCD —a very unpopular stance at that time—and was forced to resign.

Roosevelt did not ease up on her activities once the United States entered the war. Throughout the conflict, she visited American troops around the world and improved morale. She went to battlefronts in the South Pacific and military bases in Britain, the Caribbean, and across the United States. Always a supporter of racial equality, she pressured the U.S. Army Nurse Corps to allow African Americans into its ranks. In 1945, the corps changed its policy.

On April 12, 1945, Franklin D. Roosevelt died in Warm Springs, Georgia. Just after the end of the war, the former first lady became a delegate to the new United Nations (UN), and headed the UN's Human Rights Commission.

Roosevelt remained involved in Democratic Party politics and actively supported the newly established state of Israel and the escalating civil rights movement. She died in 1962.

ANNE FRANK

SYMBOL OF GERMAN OPPRESSION OF THE JEWS

Anne Frank, a German Jew, was born in Frankfurt in 1929. When she was five, her family moved to Amsterdam, Netherlands, to escape the Nazi persecution of Jews.

In 1942, on her thirteenth birthday, Anne was presented with a blank diary in which she might record the thoughts and events of her days. Later that year, her sixteen-year-old sister Margot was summoned to appear before the Nazis, who by then had occupied the Netherlands. Margot was scheduled to be sent off to Germany for "labor service."

For several months, the Frank family had been planning to go into hiding. Fearing for Margot's safety, they realized that the time had come to do so. The day after Margot received her summons, the Franks went into hiding in several rooms above a warehouse.

The Frank family—Anne, Margot, and their parents, Otto and Edith—and four others remained in the rooms for the next twenty-five months. Several friends assisted them and brought them food and news of the outside world. During this time, Anne maintained her diary. In it, she expressed with honesty and clarity her adolescent hopes, moods, feelings, and yearnings just as any young teenager might. The difference was that she was not free to attend school, take up hobbies, nor to socialize with schoolmates.

With the publication of the diary (above) she kept while in hiding with her family in the Netherlands during German occupation, Anne Frank (opposite page) became a symbol of Jewish oppression during World War II.

In 1944, the Franks and their friends were betrayed and dispatched to concentration camps. Anne and Margot ended up in Germany's Bergen-Belsen camp, where they died of typhus in 1945. Edith Frank died at the Auschwitz-Birkenau camp in Poland. The others in hiding with the Franks also perished. Only Otto Frank survived the war; he died in 1980.

Of the millions who lost their lives in Hitler's concentration camps, Anne Frank is perhaps the best remembered, because her diary was found and published as *Anne Frank: Diary of a Young Girl* (1947). It was translated into sixty-seven languages and adapted into a stage play (1955) and several motion pictures and television programs.

HARRY S. TRUMAN

ORDERED THE USE OF THE ATOMIC BOMBS

Harry Truman was born on a farm in Lamar, Missouri, in 1884. In 1934, he was elected U.S. senator. He solidified his national reputation in 1940, when he spearheaded an investigation into corruption in the government's defense industry. In 1944, Truman became the running mate of President Franklin Roosevelt. After Roosevelt's sudden death in April 1945, Truman found himself president of a nation still at war.

U.S. president Harry S. Truman (opposite page) was sworn into office (above) hours after Franklin D. Roosevelt's death. Truman's presidency is marked by his decision to drop atomic bombs on Hiroshima and Nagasaki.

Truman headed the U.S. government at the German surrender, pushed for the establishment of the United Nations, and conferred with Allied leaders on postwar policies. His most momentous wartime action, however, involved his controversial decision to authorize use of the atomic bomb over Hiroshima and Nagasaki in Japan. At the time, the Allies were winning the war in the Pacific, taking over island after island from the Japanese. An invasion of Japan seemed imminent. It appeared to be the only way in which the Allies finally would defeat Japan. Such an invasion, however, would result in countless Allied casualties.

Truman decided to employ the atom bomb to avoid these losses. One was dropped over Hiroshima on August 6, 1945. A second was dropped over Nagasaki on August 9. The invasion thus was avoided, and on September 2, Japan surrendered to the Allies. Although Truman's actions shortened the war, the bombs caused horrific destruction and the result was shocking. More than 170,000 Japanese were killed by the blasts.

After the war, Truman offered financial aid to assist those nations recovering from the war. He was narrowly reelected in 1948, sent U.S. troops to fight in the Korean War (1950–1953), and decided not to run for reelection in 1952. He died in 1972.

1919	Adolf Hitler joins the German Worker's Party, which becomes the National Socialist (Nazi) Party.
1919, June 28	The signing of the Treaty of Versailles, which ends World War I (1914–1918), leaves Germans irate and the country's economy in shambles.
1921	Benito Mussolini organizes the Fascist Party.
1933, January	Adolf Hitler becomes chancellor of Germany.
1938, September 30	British, French, German, and Italian leaders sign the Munich Agreement to give part of Czechoslovakia to Germany.
1939, August 23	Hitler signs a nonaggression pact with Stalin.
September 1	Hitler invades Poland.
September 3	France, Britain, Australia, and New Zealand declare war on Germany.
September 5	United States declares its neutrality in the new European war.
September 17	Russia invades Poland.
September 29	The Germans and Russians divide up Poland.
1940, May–June	Germany invades and takes over the Low Countries (Belgium, the Netherlands, and Luxembourg) and France.
May 27–June 4	Over 330,000 British and Allied troops are evacuated from Dunkirk (Dunkerque), a northern French seaport.
June 14	Hitler's armies march into Paris.
June 18	In a radio broadcast from Britain, Charles de Gaulle urges the French to resist the Nazi invaders. The Free French movement is born.
June 22	Pétain signs an armistice with the Nazis.
August 8–October 31	Britain's Royal Air Force (RAF) and Germany's Luftwaffe face each other in the Battle of Britain; Germany bombs Britain's major cities.
September 27	Japan joins Germany and Italy in the Axis alliance.
1941, June 22	Germany invades Russia.
December 7	The Japanese launch a surprise attack on the American military base at Pearl Harbor.

December 8	The United States and Britain declare war on Japan.
December 11	Germany and Italy declare war on the United States.
1943, July 25	Sicily falls to the Allies, which forces Mussolini out of power.
September 8	Italy surrenders to the Allies.
1944, June 6 (D-day)	The invasion of Nazi-occupied France begins with 156,000 Allied soldiers landing on a thirty-mile stretch of Normandy beaches.
August 4	Anne Frank, her family members, and friends in hiding are arrested by the Gestapo in Amsterdam, Netherlands.
August 24	The Free French reenter Paris; Charles de Gaulle's temporary government takes power in liberated France.
October 23	The United States, Britain, and Russia acknowledge the authority of Charles de Gaulle's provisional government in France.
December 16	In what came to be known as the Battle of the Bulge, the Germans mount an offensive in the Ardennes in northern France, Luxembourg, and southeastern Belgium. It is their final offensive of the war, and is a failure.
1945, April	Philippe Pétain is arrested and charged with treason; his death sentence eventually is commuted to life in prison.
April–June	Representatives of fifty-six nations attend the San Francisco Conference, which results in the formation of the United Nations.
April 28	Mussolini is killed by Italian partisans.
April 30	Hitler commits suicide in his bunker in Berlin.
May 2	Russians troops gain complete control of Berlin.
May 7	All German forces surrender unconditionally to the Allies.
July 1	United States, British, and French troops join the Russians in Berlin.
August 6	United States drops an atomic bomb over Hiroshima, Japan.
August 9	A second atomic bomb is dropped over Nagasaki, Japan.
September 2	Japan surrenders to the Allies, ending World War II.
November 20	The Nuremberg war crimes trials begin.
1946	Emperor Hirohito approves a new Japanese democratic constitution.

For Further Information

Books

Stephen Ambrose, *The Good Fight: How World War II Was Won*. New York: Atheneum, 2001.

Sean Connolly, *World War II*. Chicago: Heinemann Library, 2003.

John Devaney, *Hitler, Mad Dictator of World War II*. New York: Putnam, 1972.

Russel Freedman, *Eleanor Roosevelt: A Life of Discovery*. New York: Clarion, 1993.

Alison Leslie Gold, *Memories of Anne Frank: Reflections of a Childhood Friend*. New York: Scholastic, 1997.

Christine Hatt, *World War II: 1939–45*. New York: Franklin Watts, 2001.

William W. Lace, *The Atom Bomb*. San Diego: Lucent, 2002.

———, *The Death Camps*. San Diego: Lucent, 1998.

———, *Leaders and Generals: World War II*. San Diego: Lucent, 2000.

———, *The Nazis*. San Diego: Lucent, 1998.

Scott Marquette, *World War II*. Vero Beach, FL: Rourke, 2003.

Nancy Robinson Masters, *Airplanes of World War II*. Mankato, MN: Capstone, 1998.

Patricia McKissack and Frederick McKissack, *Red-Tail Angels: The Story of the Tuskegee Airmen of World War II*. New York: Walker, 2001.

Don Nardo, *World War II in the Pacific*. San Diego: Lucent, 2002.

William L. O'Neill, *World War II: A Student Companion*. New York: Oxford University Press, 1999.

Fiona Reynoldson, *Key Battles of World War II*. Chicago: Heinemann Library, 2001.

Earle Rice Jr., *The Attack on Pearl Harbor*. San Diego: Lucent, 1997.

Anne Grenn Saldinger, *Life in a Nazi Concentration Camp*. San Diego: Lucent, 2000.

R. Conrad Stein, *World War II in the Pacific: "Remember Pearl Harbor."* Hillside, N J: Enslow, 1994.

John F. Wukovits, *Life of an American Soldier in Europe: World War II*. San Diego: Lucent, 2000.

FOR FURTHER INFORMATION

WEBSITES

BBC History: World War II
www.bbc.co.uk
This expansive web page chronicles the history of World War II from a British perspective. It features an array of World War II–related material, including articles about the war's battles, veteran reminiscences, a gallery of child survivors of the Holocaust, examples of Nazi propaganda, and an audio of Winston Churchill.

Rutgers Oral History Archives of World War II
http://fas-history.rutgers.edu
Its website features scores of interviews of individuals who lived during World War II.

Second World War Encyclopaedia
www.spartacus.schoolnet.co.uk
This website includes scores of World War II links, under two dozens headings ranging from "Background to the War" to "Weapons and Tactics."

World War II
http://members.aol.com
This website features links to an array of World War II information, from African Americans in the war, appeasement, and atomic weapons, to V-E Day, V-J Day, war crimes indictments, and women's roles in the war.

World War II: The Homefront
http://library.thinkquest.org
This website spotlights life in the United States during World War II.

World War II Links on the Internet
http://history.acusd.edu
This website consists of scores of links to World War II–related subjects, from "A-bomb" and "Aviation" to "Espionage" and "Holocaust" to "Propaganda" and "United States Military &; Units."

# ABOUT THE AUTHOR

Audrey Kupferberg is a writer and film historian who teaches at the University at Albany. She lives in Amsterdam, New York, with her husband, Rob Edelman, with whom she has authored books on movie and television personalities. She enjoys playing racquetball and golf.